John
Leader Guide

John
The Gospel of Light and Life

John: The Gospel of Light and Life
978-1-501-80533-2
978-1-501-80534-9 eBook

John: Large Print Edition
978-1-501-80535-6

John: Leader Guide
978-1-501-80536-3
978-1-501-80537-0 eBook

John: DVD
978-1-501-80541-7

John: Youth Study Book
978-1-501-80548-6
978-1-5018-0549-3 eBook

John: Children's Leader Guide
978-1-501-80550-9

For more information, visit www.AdamHamilton.org.

Also by Adam Hamilton

24 Hours That Changed the World

Christianity and World Religions

Christianity's Family Tree

Confronting the Controversies

Enough

Final Words from the Cross

Forgiveness

Leading Beyond the Walls

Love to Stay

Making Sense of the Bible

Not a Silent Night

Revival

Seeing Gray in a World of Black and White

Selling Swimsuits in the Arctic

Speaking Well

The Call

The Journey

The Way

Unleashing the Word

When Christians Get It Wrong

Why?

ADAM HAMILTON

Author of *The Way, The Journey,* and *24 Hours That Changed the World*

JOHN
The Gospel of Light and Life

Leader Guide
by Clara Welch

Abingdon Press / Nashville

John:
The Gospel of Light and Life

Leader Guide
by Clara Welch

This book is printed on elemental chlorine-free paper.

ISBN 978-1-5018-0536-3

15 16 17 18 19 20 21 22 23 24—10 9 8 7 6 5 4 3 2 1

MANUFACTURED IN THE UNITED STATES OF AMERICA

CONTENTS

TO THE LEADER

Welcome! Thank you for accepting the invitation to serve as the facilitator for this study. You and your group of learners will journey together toward a stronger and deeper relationship with Jesus Christ.

There are two themes tying the six sessions of this study together, and those themes are expressed in the title of Adam Hamilton's book: light and life. John wrote in the prologue to his Gospel that Jesus Christ is "the light for all people" (John1:4). And toward the end of his Gospel John tells us that "these things are written so that you will believe that Jesus is the Christ, God's Son, and that believing, you will have life in his name" (John 20:31). Throughout the study, participants will be invited to reflect on these two themes as related to their own lives.

In the first session we will focus on the prologue to the Gospel and discover what it reveals about Jesus. In the next two sessions we will be encouraged to look for deeper layers of meaning in the stories of Jesus' miraculous signs and the "I AM" sayings. The fourth session focuses on Jesus' Farewell Discourse on the night of the Last Supper with his disciples. The events of Jesus' arrest, trial, and crucifixion will be the subject of the fifth session. In the sixth and final session, we will celebrate the Resurrection and eternal life.

One goal of this study is to have each participant read the entire Gospel of John. The Gospel has been divided into six parts, and one of these parts has been included after each chapter of Adam Hamilton's book. If participants read one part along with the book chapter each week, by the end of the study they will have finished the Gospel of John. Reading the Gospel in this way can provide a valuable Lenten discipline.

This six-session study for adults makes use of these components:

- the study book *John: The Gospel of Light and Life,* by Adam Hamilton;
- a DVD in which Hamilton, using stories and Scripture, presents and expands upon key points from the book;
- this Leader Guide.

Participants in the study will need Bibles. If possible, notify those interested in the study in advance of the first session. Make arrangements for them to get copies of the book so that they can read Chapter 1.

For those who would like to have an all-church emphasis on the Gospel of John, the program includes a Youth Study Book and a Children's Leader Guide so that all ages can be involved.

Using This Guide with Your Group

Scripture tells us that where two or three are gathered together, we can be assured of the presence of the Holy Spirit working in and through all those gathered. As you prepare to lead, pray for that presence and expect that you will experience it.

Because no two groups are alike, this guide has been designed to give you, as study leader, some flexibility and choice in tailoring the sessions for your group. The session format is listed below.

In the book and videos, participants will discover a rich offering of information presented in an accessible way. As study leader, you will want to tailor your session activities to the needs and interests of your particular group, as well as to the time frame you have available.

Session Format

Planning the Session
    Session Goals
    Biblical Foundation
    Before the Session

Getting Started
    Opening Activities
    Opening Prayer
Learning Together
    Video Study and Discussion
    Bible and Book Study and Discussion
    Hymn Study and Discussion
Wrapping Up
    Closing Activity
    Closing Prayer

Helpful Hints

Preparing for the Session

- Pray for the leading of the Holy Spirit as you prepare for the study. Pray for discernment for yourself and for each member of the study group.
- Before each session, familiarize yourself with the content. Read the week's book chapters again and watch the video segment.
- Choose the session elements you will use during the group session, including the specific discussion questions you plan to cover. Be prepared, however, to adjust the session as group members interact and as questions arise. Prepare carefully, but allow space for the Holy Spirit to move through the group members and through you as facilitator.
- Secure a TV and DVD player in advance.
- Prepare the space where the session will be held so that it will enhance the learning process. Ideally, group members should be seated around a table or in a circle so that all can see each other. Movable chairs are best, because the group may form pairs or small groups for discussion.
- Bring a supply of Bibles for those who forget to bring their own. Having a variety of translations is helpful.
- For most sessions you will also need a chalkboard and chalk, a whiteboard and markers, or an easel with paper and markers.

Shaping the Learning Environment

- Create a climate of openness, encouraging group members to participate as they feel comfortable. Remember that some persons will jump right in with answers and comments, while others need time to process what is being discussed.
- If you notice that some group members never seem able to enter the conversation, ask them if they have thoughts to share. Give everyone a chance to talk, but keep the conversation moving. Moderate to prevent a few individuals from doing all the talking.
- Communicate the importance of group discussions and group exercises.
- If no one answers at first during discussions, do not be afraid of a silence. Count silently to ten; then say something such as, "Would anyone like to go first?" If no one responds, venture an answer yourself and ask for comments.
- Model openness as you share with the group. Group members will follow your example. If you limit your sharing to a surface level, others will do the same.
- Encourage multiple answers or responses before moving on.
- To help continue a discussion and give it greater depth, ask, "Why?" or "Why do you believe that?" or "Can you say more about that?"
- Affirm others' responses with comments such as "Great" or "Thanks" or "Good insight"—especially if this is the first time someone has spoken during the group session.
- Monitor your own contributions. If you are doing most of the talking, back off so that you do not train the group to listen rather than speak up.
- Remember that you do not have all the answers. Your job is to keep the discussion going and encourage participation.

Managing the Session

- Begin and end on time. If a session is running longer than expected, get consensus from the group before continuing beyond the agreed-upon ending time.
- Involve group members in various aspects of the group session, such as playing the DVD, saying prayers, or reading from Scripture.

- Note that some sessions may call for breaking into smaller groups or pairs. This gives everyone a chance to speak and participate fully. Mix up the groups; encourage everyone not to pair up with the same person for every activity.
- The study will be most successful if group members treat one another with respect and are willing to listen to opinions that differ from their own. Work to ensure that the study offers a safe space for exploring the Bible.

1

THE WORD MADE FLESH

Planning the Session

Session Goals

Through conversation, activities, and reflection, participants will:

- Identify what makes the Gospel of John unique in comparison with the Synoptic Gospels
- Explore the meaning of *Logos* or "the Word" in John's Gospel
- Understand the significance of the Incarnation
- Consider our various experiences of "darkness"
- Recognize how Jesus Christ is the light that overcomes the darkness
- Discover some ways in which Jesus Christ offers us life
- Discern what it means to put our trust in Jesus Christ
- Celebrate how Jesus Christ is our light and life

Biblical Foundation

In the beginning was the Word and the Word was with God and the Word was God. The Word was with God in the beginning. Everything came into being through the Word, and without the Word nothing came into being. What came into being through the Word was life, and the life was the light for all people. The light shines in the darkness and the darkness doesn't extinguish the light. (John 1:1-5)

The Word became flesh and made his home among us. (John 1:14)

No one has ever seen God. God the only Son, who is at the Father's side, has made God known. (John 1:18)

Before the Session

- Set up a table in the room with name tags, markers, Bibles, and extra copies of *John: The Gospel of Light and Life.*
- On a large sheet of paper, whiteboard, or chalkboard write the heading: "John: The Gospel of Light and Life."
- On another large sheet of paper, whiteboard, or chalkboard make two columns, one titled "Synoptics" and one titled "John."
- Have markers or chalk available for recording participant responses.
- On a large sheet of paper, write the focus questions for passages from John as stated in Hamilton's book and display them in the room for each session during the study.
  - What is said in this passage about Jesus?
  - In this passage, how does Jesus bring life to me?
  - What response do these verses require of me?
- For the Word Made Flesh activity, bring a Bible commentary, a Bible dictionary, and a concordance. Make sure these include a listing for *Logos,* "the Word," or "the Word of God." Write the instructions as included in the session plan on a large sheet of paper, whiteboard, or chalkboard, or print the instructions on papers to distribute to the group members.
- If you plan to do the Hymn Study activity, collect hymnals that include the hymn "'Tis So Sweet to Trust in Jesus."
- Have paper and pencils available in case any participants need them for the journaling activity at the end of the session.

- Cut printer paper into strips or collect three-by-five cards for the Closing Activity: Create a Litany of Celebration.
- **Remember that there are more activities than most groups will have time to complete. As leader, you'll want to go over the session in advance and select or adapt the activities you think will work best for your group in the time allotted.**

Getting Started

Opening Activities

Greet participants as they arrive. Invite them to make a name tag and to pick up a Bible or copy of *John: The Gospel of Light and Life* if they did not bring one.

Introduce yourself. You may want to share why you are excited about teaching this Bible study.

If you sense that the participants in your group do not know each other well, allow time for them to introduce themselves and share something about their relationship with the church—for example, the name of a Sunday school class or small group to which they belong, a mission project they support, or which worship service they attend. Extend a special welcome to anyone who does not regularly attend your church, and invite them to worship at your church if they do not have a church home.

Housekeeping

- Share any necessary information about your meeting space and parking.
- Let participants know you will be faithful to the time and encourage everyone to arrive on time.
- Encourage participants to read the upcoming chapter each week and do any "homework" that may be suggested.
- Encourage participants to purchase a notebook or journal for the study. Explain that the notebook or journal may be used to record questions and insights they have as they read the chapter each week. There will be time for reflection and journaling at the end of each session. Explain that what they write in the journal will be

confidential, but they will have opportunities to share from their journals.

- Ask participants to covenant together that they will respect a policy of confidentiality within the group.

Lenten Discipline

Share the idea of reading the entire Gospel of John during this season as a Lenten discipline. Note that the text of John's Gospel, divided into six manageable parts, is included in the study book to encourage this discipline.

Read the first sentence of the introduction to the book: "John is unique among the Gospels."

Draw attention to the heading on the paper or board: "John: The Gospel of Light and Life." Invite participants to share

- a word or phrase that describes the Gospel of John for them.
- a word or phrase that describes a personal feeling or impression of the Gospel of John.

Write the words and phrases on the paper or board. Place check marks after words and phrases that are suggested by more than one person.

Opening Prayer

Holy God of light and life, thank you for your Son, Jesus Christ. Thank you for Jesus' follower who so long ago wrote the words of this Gospel so that we might know Jesus Christ and live in relationship with him. Bless our time together as we study this Gospel. Open our hearts so that we may be receptive to your word. In Jesus' name we pray. Amen.

Learning Together

Video Study and Discussion

Adam Hamilton makes introductory remarks about the Gospel of John and invites us to consider the question "What does Jesus mean?" In other words, does Jesus' life change anything for you?

After viewing the video, invite the group to discuss these questions:

- Who may have written the Gospel of John?
- Has your understanding of who Jesus is, and your relationship with Jesus, changed since you first learned about Jesus?
- What are some differences between the Gospel of John and the three Synoptic Gospels?
- What stories and texts in the three Synoptic Gospels can you recall that teach what it means to follow Jesus?
- In the Gospel of John, what does Jesus call us to do?
- What is Adam's challenge for us this week? ("Bear the light of Christ into this dark world.") What are some ways we can meet that challenge?

Bible and Book Study and Discussion

Introduction

Review Hamilton's opening sentence, "John is unique among the Gospels." Remind the group that the other three Gospels are referred to as the Synoptic Gospels. Explain that *synoptic* means "to see together" in Greek.

Invite participants to use information from the Introduction to note differences between the Synoptic Gospels and the Gospel of John. Record the responses in the appropriate column on the paper or board. Ask:

- Who wrote the Gospel of John?
- When was the Gospel of John written?
- What is the central question addressed in this Gospel?

Call attention to the three questions you have displayed in the room. Invite participants to keep these in mind as they read the Gospel of John. Read the closing paragraph of the introduction.

The Word Made Flesh

Invite a volunteer to read John 1:1-3. Ask:

- What is the premise of the Gospel of John, as introduced in the prologue? ("Jesus embodies God's Word.")
- What is the Greek term that John uses for "the Word"? (*Logos*)

17

- What does "the Word" or *Logos* mean as it is used in John's Gospel? (Suggestions from the study book include "logic and logical" and also "God's heart, God's reasoning, God's mind, God's purposes, God's character, God's desire to communicate and create.")

Divide the group into three smaller groups. Give one group a Bible commentary, one group a Bible dictionary, and one group a concordance. Call attention to the activity instructions displayed in the room, or distribute the written instructions to each group.

- Bible commentary: Look up John 1:1-18. Note additional insights regarding the meaning of the Greek word *Logos*.
- Bible dictionary: Look up "the Word" and note various ways the term is used in the Bible. (Be sure the Bible dictionary you selected includes information on "the Word." Some do not.)
- Concordance: Look up Scripture passages that reference "the Word of God." Identify verses that use "the Word" in the same context as John's Gospel and verses that use "the Word" in a different context.

Afterward, allow time for each of the smaller groups to share its findings with the large group.

Read John 1:14. Note Hamilton's statement: "The premise of the Bible is that the God who created the universe wants to be known by human beings."

Using information from the book, briefly define the doctrine of the Incarnation. Ask: Why is the doctrine of the Incarnation important for our Christian faith? (This may be a free discussion, as participants share personal understandings, experiences, and questions.)

Light Shining in the Darkness

Invite a volunteer to read John 1:3-5. Note that Hamilton describes "darkness" in several ways: spiritual blindness, failure to understand what it means to be human, despair, hopelessness, evil. Ask:

- How do you describe darkness?
- How have you experienced darkness?
- Where is there darkness in our church, our community, and around the world?

- What does John say about light in the prologue?
- How does Jesus bring light into your life?
- How can we "knock holes in the darkness" and be the light of Christ for others, both as individuals and as the church?

In Him Was Life

Read John 20:31, and note that in this verse John gives a reason for writing this Gospel.

Invite participants to recite John 3:16. Martin Luther called this the "Gospel in miniature." Discuss:

- What does "eternal life" mean in John's Gospel? (Hamilton makes the point that eternal life does not only mean life after death. It also means the experience of new life in Christ during our earthly lives.)
- How have you experienced the reality that eternal life begins now in our life on earth?

Invite a volunteer to read John 5:24. Ask:

- How have you "passed from death into life" in your life here on earth?
- What does it mean to have new life in Christ?

Read the quotation from Russell D. Moore and invite participants to respond. Ask:

- What is the difference between inviting Christ into your life and accepting Christ's invitation into his life?

In Jesus' Arms

Note: As you lead this discussion about trust, be mindful that not everyone is at the same place in their Christian faith. Some participants in your group may have learned to trust God through a variety of challenging circumstances. Other participants may feel as though their trust is shaky or tentative or that God let them down at some point. Even the strongest Christians sometimes falter in the darkness. You may want to share the story of Peter, who walked on the water toward Jesus. When he lost focus on Jesus, "he became frightened." He called out, "Lord, rescue me!" (Matthew 14:30). The text says, "Jesus immediately reached out and grabbed him" (Matthew 14:31). God loves us even when our trust is fragile. God is trustworthy even when we have doubts.

Share Hamilton's invitation at the end of this section for us to trust: "I'd like to invite you to trust in Christ...who offers light and life to all who believe." Discuss:

- In what ways have you put your trust in Jesus Christ?
- Are there areas of your life where you do not trust in Christ? If there are, what holds you back?
- When you find yourself in darkness, what does it mean to trust Jesus to be your light and life? (You may want to refer back to examples of darkness previously shared to guide this discussion.)

Hymn Study and Discussion

Distribute hymnals that include the hymn "'Tis So Sweet to Trust in Jesus." Read or sing the words together. Invite participants to share phrases in the hymn that speak to them. Ask:

- How does this phrase speak to you or describe your experience of trusting Jesus?

Before you close the discussion, call attention to the last phrase if it has not been mentioned: "O for grace to trust him more!" Note that this phrase reminds us we are all growing in our faith.

Wrapping Up

Closing Activities

John's Gospel Speaks to Us

Pose two questions for participants to think about, given what they have read and learned so far.

- Specifically, what do I want to explore or work on this week?
- What questions do I still have about the prologue to John's Gospel and the topics we discussed?

- Allow time for participants to reflect and journal on these questions. Distribute paper and a pencil to anyone who needs them for journaling. Invite anyone who would like to, to share responses, new insights, and questions they have as a result of this session together.

Create a Litany of Celebration

Explain that the word *gospel* as used in this study has two meanings: (1) the good tidings or good news of Jesus Christ, and (2) the books that tell the story of Jesus Christ: Matthew, Mark, Luke, and John (when capitalized).

John's prologue announces the good tidings that Jesus is both our light and our life. Ask participants to read John 1:1-14 silently or invite a volunteer to read these verses aloud.

Distribute strips of paper or three-by-five cards and invite participants to work individually or in pairs to write one or more sentences for a litany. The sentence may begin with either, "I celebrate…" or "Thank you…." Note that the group response for the litany will be "Thank you, God, for light and life."

After participants have had the opportunity to write sentences for the litany, collect the papers or cards. Invite the class to enter into a time of worship. Read each sentence separately with a voice of celebration and invite participants to offer praise to God by responding after each sentence with the words "Thank you, God, for light and life."

Remind participants to engage in the Lenten discipline of reading a portion of John's Gospel each week.

Closing Prayer

Invite participants to say the prayer at the end of Chapter 1 in the study book aloud together.

Jesus, I trust in you, that you are God's Word in the flesh. I trust that you are the light of the world. Illuminate my darkness. Help me to walk in your light and to love and follow you all of my days. In your holy name. Amen.

2

THE MIRACULOUS SIGNS OF JESUS

Planning the Session

Session Goals

Through conversation, activities, and reflection, participants will:

- Explore the meaning in John's story of Jesus changing water into wine.
- Explore the meaning in John's story of Jesus healing the blind beggar.
- Affirm belief and trust in Christ, recognizing that each believer grows in trust throughout the journey of faith.
- Consider what Christ calls us to do.
- Examine suffering from the perspective that God can use our suffering to reveal God's glory.
- Reflect on our own spiritual blindness and recognize our need for healing.

Biblical Foundation

On the third day there was a wedding in Cana of Galilee. Jesus' mother was there, and Jesus and his disciples were also invited to the celebration. When the wine ran out, Jesus' mother said to him, "They don't have any wine." Jesus replied, "Woman, what does that have to do with me? My time hasn't come yet." His mother told the servants, "Do whatever he tells you."

(John 2:1-5)

As Jesus walked along, he saw a man who was blind from birth. Jesus' disciples asked, "Rabbi, who sinned so that he was born blind, this man or his parents?" Jesus answered, "Neither he nor his parents. This happened so that God's mighty works might be displayed in him." (John 9:1-3)

Before the Session

- Write the heading "Water into Wine" on a board or large sheet of paper.
- Write the heading "Healing the Blind Beggar" on another board or large sheet of paper.
- Have markers or chalk and a board or paper available to record participant's responses during the session.
- You may want to locate a print or online image of Vincent van Gogh's painting *The Starry Night* and display it in the room.
- Collect hymnals that contain the hymn "Amazing Grace" or have a recording available. Another idea is to invite a singer in your group to be prepared to sing "Amazing Grace" as a solo at the end of the session. Invite this person several days in advance.
- **Remember that there are more activities than most groups will have time to complete. As leader, you'll want to go over the session in advance and select or adapt the activities you think will work best for your group in the time allotted.**

Getting Started

Opening Activities

Greet participants as they arrive. Review any instructions from Session 1 that you feel need to be repeated. Remind participants of the importance of confidentiality.

Draw attention to the heading "Water into Wine" on the board or paper. Invite participants to call out the first words, phrases, or questions that come to mind when they think of the story about Jesus changing the water into wine. Record the responses randomly on the board or paper, without comment. Responses may include: wedding, miracle, best for last.

Then draw attention to the board or paper with the heading "Healing the Blind Beggar." Again, invite participants to call out the first words, phrases, or questions that come to mind when they think of this story and record the responses randomly on the paper, without comment. Responses may include: who sinned? accusing bystanders, mud, new life.

Opening Prayer

Holy God of light and life, thank you for your son, Jesus Christ. Thank you for these stories written so long ago. Open our minds as we consider these stories so that we may grow in our understanding of who Jesus is and who you call us to be. Open our hearts that we may hear and receive your word and live faithfully as your children. In Jesus' name we pray, Amen.

Learning Together

Video Study and Discussion

Seven "miraculous signs" are recorded in John's Gospel. The stories of these miraculous signs may be read on two levels: a surface level and a deeper level.

After viewing the video, invite the group to discuss these questions:

- Why is it important to pay attention to the details when we read the Gospel of John?
- What miraculous signs have you experienced in your life?
- Where is spiritual blindness evident in our world today? How can we as the church respond to this spiritual blindness?
- Why did John write this Gospel? (See John 20:30-31.)
- What does it mean to have life in Jesus' name?

Bible and Book Study and Discussion

Miraculous Signs

The first twelve chapters of John contain stories of seven miracles that Jesus performed during his ministry on earth. John calls these miracles "miraculous signs."

Explain that the stories of the "miraculous signs" may be read on two levels: (1) a straightforward level that follows the actions of the story, and (2) a deeper level that reveals the nature of Christ and invites us into a relationship with Christ.

You may want to share Hamilton's description of the painting *The Starry Night* by Vincent van Gogh. Invite participants to share thoughts and insights about the painting.

Water into Wine

Invite four volunteers to read John 2:1-12, assigning parts to each volunteer as follows: narrator, Jesus, Jesus' mother, headwaiter. Explain that they will read the Scripture passage twice, allowing time for discussion after each reading. The first time will serve as a practice reading. The second reading should be a more thoughtful performance.

After the first reading, ask the following fact-based questions:

- Who are the characters in this story?
- What does each character do in the story?

After the second reading, ask the following questions that require examining the story in more depth:

- Why do you think it is significant that this story takes place at a wedding party? (Jesus used the illustration of a wedding party in other teachings. You may want to read or invite volunteers to read Jesus' parables in Matthew 22:1-10, Matthew 25:1-13, and Luke 12:35-40. Wedding imagery is also present in Revelation 19:7-10 and 21:1-3.)
- What is the significance of the instruction to "Do whatever he tells you"? Consider the meaning both in the story and in our lives today.

- Why might John have offered the detail that the water jars were made of "stone"? (You may want to read Ezekiel 36:24-27. These verses are part of God's promise to deliver the people of Israel and Judah from exile in Babylon.)
- How does the reference to the "Jewish cleansing ritual" broaden the significance of this story?
- What does the "good wine" represent? (Responses may include a spiritual life that is characterized by forgiveness, joy, peace, and hope.)
- How does the image of jugs filled "to the brim" describe your experience of the Christian faith?

Share information from Hamilton's book about Dionysus or Bacchus, the ancient Greek or Roman god of wine and mirth. Ask:

- How does the secular world tempt us away from Christ?
- How can we resist temptation and remain in Christ?
- What does Christ offer us that the world does not?

Healing the Blind Beggar

Invite ten volunteers to read John 9 according to the parts below. If you do not have ten readers, then assign multiple parts to one or more readers. If your group is large, several people may read the parts for the disciples, neighbors, and Pharisees in unison to give the idea of a crowd being present.

- Narrator
- Disciples
- Jesus
- Neighbor
- Some (verse 9)
- Others (verse 9)
- Blind beggar
- Some Pharisees/Jewish leaders
- Other Pharisees
- Parents

Again, explain that the group will read the passage twice, allowing time for discussion after each reading. The first time will serve as a practice reading. The second reading should be a more thoughtful performance.

After the first reading ask the following fact-based questions:

- Who are the characters in the story?
- What are the main events in the story?

After the second reading, ask the following questions that require examining the story in more depth:

- Why did the disciples ask, "Who sinned?" (The question was prompted by the Jewish law; see Exodus 20:5b.)
- How is this "cause-and-effect" way of thinking still evident in our world today?

Note that Hamilton makes two points about suffering.

- Sometimes bad things happen to us as a consequence of our own actions.
- God does not punish us with hardship and suffering. Jesus suffered the punishment for our sin.

Explain that in John 9:35-38 the healed blind man did not recognize Jesus at first because he had been blind when he left Jesus to go wash in the pool of Siloam. Discuss:

- How are people spiritually blind today?
- How can we as followers of Christ help heal people's spiritual blindness?
- How does the blind beggar in this story represent each of us?

Hymn Study and Discussion

Distribute hymnals that include the hymn "Amazing Grace." Recall the story behind this hymn as shared in the study book. Invite participants to be in an attitude of worship as the group sings or reads together the words of the hymn together. Alternatively, play a recording of the hymn or listen as a soloist sings the hymn.

- What does the word *grace* mean to you?
- How is the meaning of the word affected, changed, or deepened by its use in the hymn?
- Consider and share examples of dramatic changes in people's lives or your own life. What role, if any, did grace play in those changes?

Wrapping Up

Closing Activities

John's Gospel Speaks to Us

Call attention to the boards or sheets of paper where you recorded the group's responses during the Opening Activities. Ask:

- After this group session, what new insights do you have?
- What questions have been answered?
- What new questions do you have for further exploration?
- How has your understanding of these stories changed or expanded through our study?

Hamilton points out that John recorded these stories to show us that Christ offers us life. Discuss:

- In what areas of your life have you been offered "new wine"?
- In what areas of your life have you received healing from spiritual blindness?
- What does Christ call you to do in order to receive new life and healing? (Remind participants of Jesus' mother's instruction, "Do whatever he tells you," and Jesus' instruction to the blind man to wash in the pool of Siloam.)

Lenten Discipline

Encourage participants to continue the discipline of reading the Gospel of John each week. Invite participants to share their experience of this discipline so far.

Closing Prayer

God of miracles and new life, make us aware of our blindness. Grant us courage to do what you call us to do. Let us be receptive to your healing presence so that we may truly experience new life in you. Amen.

3

THE "I AM" SAYINGS OF JESUS

Planning the Session

Session Goals

Through conversation, activities, and reflection, participants will:

- Examine the significance of God's name, "I Am Who I Am."
- Explore the meaning of the seven "I AM" sayings of Jesus.
- Consider how the image of bread reminds us that Jesus Christ is our sustainer and our salvation.
- Reflect on the symbolism that Jesus is the light of the world.

Biblical Foundation

But Moses said to God, "If I now come to the Israelites and say to them, 'The God of your ancestors has sent me to you,' they are going to ask me, 'What's this God's name?' What am I supposed to say to them?" God said to Moses, "I Am Who I Am. So say to the Israelites, 'I Am has sent me to you.'" (Exodus 3:13-14)

"Your father Abraham was overjoyed that he would see my day. He saw it and was happy." "You aren't even 50 years old!" the Jewish opposition

*replied. "How can you say that you have seen Abraham?" "I assure you,"
Jesus replied, "before Abraham was, I Am." (John 8:56-58)*

Before the Session

- Have small pieces of paper and pencils ready for the opening activity, the "I AM" game.
- Write the heading "Names for God" on the board or on a large sheet of paper.
- You may want to write each of the seven "I AM" sayings on separate pieces of colored paper and post them in the room.
- Decide how you want to give information to the pairs or small groups for the Biblical Research activity. Possibilities: write the Scripture references and questions on a board or large sheet of paper for all to see; write them on four individual pieces of paper to distribute to each group; or give this information verbally.
- If you decide to do the alternative idea (marked with an *) for the Biblical Research activity, recruit and give instructions to the researchers early in the week.
- Have a candle in a candleholder and matches available for the Light Activity. If your group meets during the day, consider ways to darken the room.
- Have a board or large sheets of paper available, along with markers or chalk to record group responses.
- **Remember that there are more activities than most groups will have time to complete. As leader, you'll want to go over the session in advance and select or adapt the activities you think will work best for your group in the time allotted.**

Getting Started

Opening Activities

Greet participants as they arrive. Allow time for introductions and housekeeping items. Remind participants of the importance of confidentiality within the group.

The "I AM" Game

- Instruct participants to write three statements about themselves beginning with the words "I am." Two of the statements should be true and one should be false.

- Each person will read his or her three statements. Participants will guess which one is the false statement.
- Examples are: I am a musician. I am allergic to peanuts. I am a traveler and my favorite destination is the mountains.
- In the interest of time, if your group is large, create smaller groups for the game.

Names for God

- Invite participants to think of the various names and titles we use when we speak of God. Examples are Lord, Creator, the Almighty, Rock, Protector, and Love.
- Write the names on a board or sheet of paper under the heading "Names for God."
- You may close this activity by inviting participants to identify the name or names that hold the most meaning for them.

Opening Prayer

Holy God of light and life, thank you for your Son, Jesus Christ. Bless our time together as we study this Gospel. Open our hearts so that we may be receptive to your word and grow in our relationship with Jesus Christ. In Jesus' name we pray. Amen.

Learning Together

Video Study and Discussion

The Gospel of John records seven "I AM" sayings of Jesus. We discuss two of the sayings: "I am the bread of life" and "I am the light of the world."

After viewing the video, invite the group to discuss these questions:

- What is the difference between a "low Christology" and a "high Christology?"
- Which "Christology" most describes your understanding and relationship with Jesus Christ?
- What is the Latin word for "breaking bread?" How is this word significant in our understanding of "breaking bread" in the sacrament of Holy Communion?
- What does Adam Hamilton suggest when he notes that in our culture "bread" (and dough) are synonyms for money?

- How do you obey the call to be a light in the world? (See Matthew 5:14-16.)

Bible and Book Study and Discussion

"I AM"

Read, or invite someone to read, John 20:31. Here John states his reason for writing this Gospel.

Explain that John's Gospel contains seven "I AM" sayings about Jesus. These sayings point to the divinity of Jesus and affirm that Jesus gives life to all who believe in him. In the Greek language the words for "I am" are *ego eimi*. Discuss:

- How do we translate the Greek word *ego*? (the self, I)
- How do we translate *eimi*? (verb "to be")
- Read Exodus 3:13-15. What was the significance of the name "I Am Who I Am" in the polytheistic culture where Moses lived? What do you think is the significance of this name in our culture today?

Biblical Research

Invite participants to turn to the pages in the study book where the seven "I AM" sayings are listed. Read the "I AM" sayings.

Create four pairs or small groups. Assign a different "I AM" saying to each group, noting that the sayings about the "gate" and "good shepherd" are grouped together and that the first two sayings ("I am the bread of life" and "I am the light of the world") will be discussed later in the session by the whole group. See the activity below for the four group topics and Scripture passages.

Give each group their Scripture passages, using the method you chose in Before the Session. Instruct the pairs or small groups to read the related passages and then discuss these questions:

- What does this "I AM" saying tell us about Jesus?
- How does this saying proclaim that Jesus gives life to everyone who believes in him?
- How did Jesus build on or reinterpret Old Testament understandings of these words and phrases?
- How does this "I AM" saying speak to us today?

Invite each small group to share with the larger group three insights or important points related to their "I AM" saying or sayings.

Information for the four pairs or small groups:

Group 1

"I am the gate of the sheep." (John 10:7)
"I am the good shepherd." (John 10:11)
Larger context: John 10:1-16.

Related Old Testament references: Psalm 23; Isaiah 40:11, 56:7-8; Ezekiel 34:23.

Group 2

"I am the resurrection and the life." (John 11:25)
Larger context: John 11:17-27.

Related Old Testament references: 1 Kings 17:17-24; Isaiah 25:8, 26:19a; Ezekiel 37:1-14; Daniel 12:1-4; Hosea 6:1-3, 13:14.

Group 3

"I am the way, the truth, and the life." (John 14:6)
Larger context: John 14:1-6.

Related Old Testament references: Exodus 13:21-22; Psalm 25:4-5, 8-10; Psalm 31:5-6; Psalm 139:7-10, 24; Deuteronomy 32:4

Group 4

"I am the true vine." (John 15:1)
Larger context: John 15:1-8.

Related Old Testament references: Psalm 80:8-19; Isaiah 5:1-7.

*Alternative idea for the Biblical Research Activity: Recruit four people early in the week who will each research an "I AM" saying and give a brief report to the group. Give each researcher the Scripture references for his or her particular saying and the four questions as noted for the small group activity.

"I am the bread of life."

Hamilton points out that John relates this "I AM" saying to two significant events: Jesus feeding the multitudes and Passover. The story of Jesus feeding the multitudes is the only miracle story that is recorded in all four Gospels; you may want to have participants read the story from each of the Gospels and note any similarities and differences. Review the events of the first Passover as described in the study book.

Read John 6:26-59. Since this is a long passage, you may want to invite several participants to read a few verses each, or ask participants to skim the passage silently.

Remind participants that the Old Testament includes over two hundred references to bread. Invite three participants to read aloud the following Old Testament texts about God's gift of manna in the wilderness. (You may want to look up additional Old Testament references to bread with the help of a concordance.)

- Exodus 16:4, 15
- Nehemiah 9:15
- Psalm 78:23-24

Discuss:

- What does the saying "I am the bread of life" tell us about Jesus when considered in the context of Passover? (Jesus brings salvation for everyone.)
- What does this saying tell us about Jesus when considered in the context of manna in the wilderness? (Christ sustains us in our journey of faith.)

Note that in addition to the Old Testament contexts of Passover and manna, we also understand this "I AM" saying in the context of Holy Communion. Ask:

- When you partake in the sacrament of Holy Communion, how are you participating in Christ's story of salvation?
- How does the sacrament of Holy Communion bind people together?
- What is the significance of the phrase "breaking bread"? What does "bread" symbolize or signify in our culture? in our community of faith? in your family?
- How does the bread of Holy Communion bring you spiritual sustenance?

"I am the light of the world."

Invite participants to read the following Old Testament references about light. (You may want to look up additional Old Testament references to light with the help of a concordance.)

- Genesis 1:3, 5, 16
- Exodus 13:21
- Ps. 27:1, 56:12-13, 119:105
- Isaiah 2:5; 49:6; 60:1, 19

Discuss:

- What does "light" represent in these Old Testament texts?
- When God called Israel and Judah to be light for other nations, what did God intend for them to do?
- What is the significance of light in the Jewish Festival of Booths? (Refer to the information about this festival in the study book.)
- What does light symbolize in the Christian faith?
- How have you experienced spiritual darkness? How have you experienced the light of Christ?
- How is your faith community a light that shows nonbelievers the way to Christ?

"Light" Activity

- Place a candle on a table in the middle of the room and light it.
- Turn off lights and close blinds and curtains if necessary to darken the room.
- Instruct participants to remain silent and be mindful of their feelings during this activity.
- Invite participants to imagine that the light of the candle flame is Christ.
- Read John 8:12.
- After a few minutes, snuff out the candle.
- Allow a few minutes for the group to sit in silent darkness.
- Re-light the candle. Allow a few more minutes of silence.
- Break the silence by reading John 8:12 again.
- Turn on the lights, open curtains and blinds, snuff out the candle.

Ask:

- How did you feel during the first part of the activity when the candle was lit?
- How did you feel when the candle was snuffed out?
- How did you feel when the candle was lit again?

Wrapping Up

Closing Activities

Invite seven participants to each read one of the "I AM" sayings of Jesus from Chapter 6 in the study book. Instruct them to read the sayings in succession with only a slight break between. Ask the following questions, then offer time for reflection and journaling.

- How has your understanding of the person, purpose, and ministry of Jesus Christ grown through this study of the "I AM" sayings?
- Do any of these "I AM" sayings speak to you in a special way?
- Which of the sayings can you be for someone else?
- What new insights do you have regarding your relationship with Jesus Christ?

Encourage participants to continue the discipline of reading the Gospel of John each week.

Invite participants to share their experience of this discipline so far.

Closing Prayer

Lord Jesus, when we look at you we believe we are seeing the Father. We know that we need more than bread to live. We need you and the love, mercy, and life that you give. Be the bread of life for us. Sustain us and feed our souls. Be our light, and dispel the darkness in our lives. May your light so shine in us that others might see you through us. Amen.

4

THE FAREWELL DISCOURSE

Planning the Session

Session Goals

Through conversation, activities, and reflection, participants will:

- Explore the content of Jesus' Farewell Discourse with his disciples as recorded in the Gospel of John.
- Discover the meaning of greatness and servanthood through the teaching of Jesus.
- Affirm the presence and work of the Holy Spirit.
- Celebrate Jesus' promise of continuing presence.
- Identify ways we obey Jesus' commandment to love.
- Consider what it means to remain in Christ's love.

Biblical Foundation

"My Father is glorified when you produce much fruit and in this way prove that you are my disciples. As the Father loved me, I too have loved you. Remain in my love. If you keep my commandments, you will remain in my love, just as I kept my Father's commandments and remain in his love."

(John 15:8-10)

39

"I will ask the Father, and he will send another Companion, who will be with you forever. This Companion is the Spirit of Truth, whom the world can't receive because it neither sees him nor recognizes him. You know him, because he lives with you and will be with you." (John 14:16-17)

Before the Session

- Write the heading "Holy Spirit" on the board or large sheet of paper for use during the discussion of John 14.
- Make the board or large sheets of paper and markers or chalk available for recording participants' responses.
- Gather hymnals that include "Breathe on Me, Breath of God." Participants may use hymnals for two activities. You may also want to have a recording to play.
- Consult the topical index of a hymnal for other hymns related to the Holy Spirit, or find the words or recordings of contemporary Christian songs about the Holy Spirit.
- **Remember that there are more activities than most groups will have time to complete. As leader, you'll want to go over the session in advance and select or adapt the activities you think will work best for your group in the time allotted.**

Getting Started

Opening Activities

Greet participants as they arrive. Remind them about the importance of confidentiality within the group.

Note that the setting for chapters 13–17 in the Gospel of John is the Last Supper that Jesus shared with his disciples. These chapters are often referred to as the "Farewell Discourse." In these chapters John records the words of instruction and encouragement that Jesus wanted to leave with his disciples before his death, resurrection, and ascension.

We will focus on Jesus' words in chapters 13–15. In these chapters we sense Jesus' great love, compassion, and concern for the disciples as he prepared them for the challenges they would face as they fulfilled the call to be witnesses for Christ.

Ask:

- What words of wisdom have been passed along to you by a family member or special friend?
- How have these words influenced your life?

Opening Prayer

Holy God of light and life, thank you for your Son, Jesus Christ. Thank you for the gift of the Holy Spirit that remains with us always. As we study your Holy Word, let us be receptive to what you want to teach us. Grant us courage to live as you call us to live and to share the love of Christ with the world. In Jesus' name we pray. Amen.

Learning Together

Video Study and Discussion

Jesus says his parting words to the disciples (the Farewell Discourse). Hamilton notes that the image of bearing fruit for Christ is another way of saying we are to love each other, and we are challenged to be intentional in bearing fruit and sharing the love of Christ.

After viewing the video, invite the group to discuss these questions:

- If you had been one of Jesus' disciples, what words of assurance and instruction would you have wanted to hear from Jesus?
- Why did Jesus pray that the disciples would be one after his death and resurrection?
- What challenges do we face today as we seek to be one in Christ? In what ways have we succeeded? In what ways can we improve?
- Where and how does the church live out Jesus' call to be his disciples?
- How will you be intentional about abiding in Christ and drawing strength from Christ during the coming week?

Bible and Book Study and Discussion

Farewell Discourse: John 13

Share information about this first chapter of the Final Discourse in John's Gospel:

- The setting is the Last Supper that Jesus shared with his disciples.
- John's account differs from the account found in the three Synoptic Gospels.
- Matthew, Mark, and Luke describe in detail Jesus' breaking bread and giving the cup. The Apostle Paul was familiar with the tradition in the Synoptic Gospels and wrote about it in his letter to the church in Corinth (1 Corinthians 11:23-26).
- In contrast, John barely mentions the bread and cup (John 13:2, 26), then focuses instead on the act of Jesus washing the disciples' feet. John is the only Gospel that includes this story.
- You may want to read, or invite someone to read, 1 Corinthians 11:23-26 and John 13:2 and 26 about Jesus breaking the bread and giving the cup to his disciples.

Read, or invite someone to read, John 13:1-20. Since this is a long text, you may want to have two or more readers. Ask:

- What happens in this story?
- Which disciples are mentioned by name? (Peter and Judas)
- What do we learn about Peter in this text?
- What do we learn about Judas in this text?

Read Luke 22:24-26. Note Hamilton's suggestion that this conversation may have prompted Jesus to teach a lesson about greatness through the act of washing his disciples' feet. Discuss:

- What do we learn through these two stories about the meaning of greatness and servanthood in the kingdom of God?
- How is the disciples' attitude toward greatness, as revealed in Luke 22:24-26, evident in our world today?
- Why did Peter at first refuse to let Jesus wash his feet? Why did Peter change his mind?
- Have you ever washed the feet of another person? If yes, how did you feel about the experience?
- Have you ever had your feet washed by someone else? If yes, how did you feel about the experience?
- What acts of service in our culture today might be equated with washing feet in Jesus day?
- How and why do acts of service make us happy? (See John 13:17.)

Farewell Discourse: John 14

Share information about this second chapter in the Farewell Discourse.

- Verse 1 centers on the theme of trust.
- Verse 6 is one of the "I am" sayings.
- In these verses, Jesus begins to prepare his disciples for the fact that his time on earth is coming to an end.
- Jesus assures his disciples that he will not leave them alone. He promises the presence of the Holy Spirit.
- In verse 16 Jesus promises that God "will send another Companion, who will be with you forever."
- In verse 18 Jesus promises, "I won't leave you as orphans."
- During the following discussion of the Holy Spirit, write the various descriptive names for the Holy Spirit on a board or paper under the heading "Holy Spirit."

Ask:

- What word is used for *Companion* in your translation of the Bible? (CEB: Companion; RSV: Counselor; NIV and NRSV: Advocate; KJV: Comforter).
- Who does Jesus say the Companion is? (the Spirit of Truth)
- What is the Greek word for spirit? (*pneuma*)
- What is the Hebrew word for spirit? (*ruach*)
- How are these words translated? (breath, wind, air)
- What word for spirit is only found in John's Gospel? (*paraclete*)
- How does Hamilton define *paraclete* in relation to the Holy Spirit?

Invite someone to read Genesis 2:4b-7. Invite someone else to read John 20:22. Discuss:

- How did God give life to humankind?
- How did Jesus give the Holy Spirit to his disciples?
- How is this significant for you?
- Where else in John's Gospel has John drawn a comparison between the creation stories and the life of Jesus?
    - In most translations, Genesis 1:1 and John 1:1 begin with the same three words, "In the beginning. . . ."
    - God formed the human person from the ground. Jesus healed the blind beggar with mud made from the ground.

- In the study book, how does Hamilton describe the presence and work of the Holy Spirit in our lives?
- Are you paying attention to ways the Holy Spirit is present and at work in your life?
- How do you invite the Holy Spirit into your life? How have you experienced the Holy Spirit?

Farewell Discourse: John 15

Read, or invite someone to read, John 15:1-8. Note that this text contains one of the seven "I am" sayings in the Gospel of John that we learned about in the previous session. Ask:

- How does this "I am" saying enhance your understanding of the Holy Spirit?
- How does the Holy Spirit keep you connected to the vine, which is Christ?
- What does verse 15:5 mean in your life? ("If you remain in me and I in you, then you will produce much fruit.")
- What are examples of "fruit" that you have helped produce as you participate in the life of your faith community?

Read, or invite someone to read, John 15:9-17. Then read, or invite someone to read, Matthew 22:35-40. Discuss:

- What is the greatest commandment Jesus calls us to obey?
- What is the relationship between bearing fruit and obeying the call to love?
- What is the relationship between Jesus' promise of continuing presence through the Holy Spirit and the commandment to love?
- What is the relationship between Jesus' example of washing the disciples' feet and the call to share Christ's love with the world?
- How do you remain in Christ's love? (John 15:9-10)
- How do you obey the command to love?

Hymn Study and Discussion

Distribute hymnals that include the hymn "Breathe on Me, Breath of God." Note that this hymn is a prayer.

- Sing or read the words together, or play a recording of the hymn.
- Invite participants to share phrases that have meaning for them.

Wrapping Up

Closing Activity

Remind participants that the Gospel of John invites us into a relationship with Jesus Christ. Note that Jesus calls us to serve him—for example, by washing each other's feet, bearing fruit, and obeying the commandment to love.

Refer to the board or paper where the descriptive names for the Holy Spirit were recorded earlier in the session. Ask:

- How do these names for the Holy Spirit spark ideas for service? (We can be a "companion" by sitting with someone whose loved one is having surgery. We can be an "advocate" for children in need by supporting ministries for children. We can serve as a "counselor" on a youth retreat or be a "comforter" by visiting residents in a nursing home. The Holy Spirit is God's presence with us. We can be present for others in Christ's name.)
- How does the image of being a branch on Christ's vine spark ideas for service?
- How can you use your talents and gifts to produce fruit for Christ?
- How can you fulfill the commandment to love God and love your neighbor?

After the discussion, encourage participants either to continue a current act of service or to adopt a new area of service as a way of growing in their relationship with Christ. Your group may even want to consider adopting a group service project.

Encourage participants to continue the discipline of reading the Gospel of John each week. Invite participants to share their experience of this discipline so far.

Closing Prayer

Gracious and Holy God, thank you for the Holy Spirit, the gift of your continuing presence that remains with us always. Fill us with the Holy Spirit that leads, guides, and empowers us. Open our eyes to the ways you call us to use our talents and abilities to serve others and bear fruit for your kingdom. Let us remain in your love. Let love for you guide our actions and our speech. In the name of Jesus Christ. Amen.

5

THE ARREST, TRIAL, AND CRUCIFIXION OF THE KING

Planning the Session

Session Goals

Through conversation, activities, and reflection, participants will:

- Review the events of the arrest, trial, and crucifixion of Jesus as recorded in the Gospel of John.
- Compare the accounts in John's Gospel with the accounts in the Synoptic Gospels.
- Consider the relationship between the Jewish festival of Passover and the events of Holy Week.
- Explore the theme of Christ as King in the Gospel of John.
- Accept God's gifts of forgiveness and salvation made possible through the atoning sacrifice of Jesus Christ.
- Discern how these accounts of the arrest, trial, and crucifixion of Jesus speak to us and impact our lives.

Biblical Foundation

Pilate said to the Jewish leaders, "Here's your king." The Jewish leaders cried out, "Take him away! Take him away! Crucify him!" Pilate responded, "What? Do you want me to crucify your king?" "We have no king except the emperor," the chief priests answered. Then Pilate handed Jesus over to be crucified. The soldiers took Jesus prisoner. Carrying his cross by himself, he went out to a place called Skull Place (in Aramaic, Golgotha). That's where they crucified him—and two others with him, one on each side and Jesus in the middle. Pilate had a public notice written and posted on the cross. It read "Jesus the Nazarene, the king of the Jews." Many of the Jews read this sign, for the place where Jesus was crucified was near the city and it was written in Aramaic, Latin, and Greek. (John 19:14b-20)

Before the Session

- Write these headings on three different sheets of paper or sections of the board: "Arrest," "Trial," "Crucifixion."
- Have markers or chalk available to record responses from the group.
- Research Passover and prepare a short report about the history and meaning of this Jewish festival to share with the group, or invite a participant to do this. If you recruit someone else to do it, be sure to ask several days in advance. The observance of the first Passover is recorded in Exodus 12. Bible commentaries and dictionaries will include information about Passover.
- Read the accounts of the arrest, trial, and crucifixion of Jesus in all four Gospels to get a feel for the differences in John's Gospel.
- Be prepared to complete the sentences in the Closing Activity to start that conversation.
- Select the activities and the questions you want to use for this session carefully. You will want to allow enough time to examine all three major events and not have to leave any out. As always, keep the needs and interests of your group in mind as you plan.
- **Remember that there are more activities than most groups will have time to complete. As leader, you'll want to go over the session in advance and select or adapt the activities you think will work best for your group in the time allotted.**

Getting Started

Opening Activities

Greet participants as they arrive. Allow time for introductions and housekeeping items. Remind participants of the importance of confidentiality within the group.

Call attention to the three headings posted: "Arrest," "Trial," "Crucifixion." Ask the following three questions and record responses under the headings, as a way for participants to see what they remember before beginning the session. Do not be concerned about writing the events in chronological order for this activity.

- What actions took place and what words were spoken during the arrest of Jesus?
- What actions took place and what words were spoken during the trial of Jesus?
- What actions took place and what words were spoken during the crucifixion of Jesus?

Opening Prayer

Holy God of light and life, thank you for your Son, Jesus Christ, who was willing to suffer and die for our salvation. Bless our time together as we study this Gospel. Open our hearts so that we may be receptive to your word. In Jesus' name we pray. Amen.

Learning Together

Video Study and Discussion

In presenting Jesus' arrest, trial, and crucifixion, John focuses on Jesus' royalty and kingship, in contrast to the Synoptic Gospels that focus on Jesus' humanity.

After viewing the video, invite the group to discuss these questions:

- What are some ways we can reconcile the differences between John's Gospel and the Synoptic Gospels with respect to time and sequence of events during Holy Week?

- What do you think Jesus meant by his last statement from the cross, "It is finished" (John 19:30 NRSV), since the Resurrection had not yet happened? In other words, what was finished?
- Why did John see the Crucifixion as Jesus' moment of glorification? What do you see as Jesus' moment of glorification?
- How do the Synoptic Gospels—emphasizing Jesus' humanity— contribute to your understanding of Jesus' arrest, trial, and crucifixion?
- How does John's Gospel—emphasizing Jesus' kingship and royalty—contribute to your understanding of Jesus' arrest, trial, and crucifixion?

Bible and Book Study and Discussion

The Arrest of Jesus

Remind participants that the Scripture passages studied in the last session were from Jesus' Farewell Discourse with his disciples at the Last Supper, just before he was arrested. To learn what happened next, read or invite someone to read John 18:1-14. Point out that John's account is somewhat different from accounts in the Synoptic Gospels.

Call attention to the list created during this session's Opening Activities of the events related to the arrest. Circle the events that are recorded in John's Gospel (as opposed to the Synoptic Gospels). Note any events in John's Gospel that were not mentioned by the group. Ask:

- What is the significance of Jesus' answer "I am"?

Note Hamilton's observation that the Synoptic Gospels emphasize the humanity of Jesus, while John's Gospel emphasizes the divinity of Jesus. Discuss:

- How do Jesus' appearance and actions in this account support John's purpose of revealing Jesus' divinity?

Create three small groups and assign each group a name: Matthew, Mark, Luke. Instruct each group to read the story of the arrest in its assigned Gospel. Scripture texts are Matthew 26:36-56; Mark 14:32-52; Luke 22:39-53. (In the interest of time, suggest that individuals skim the Scriptures silently instead of one person reading the text aloud.)

Ask each group to note similarities and differences between their Gospel account and John's account. Allow time for each small group to share its findings with the whole group. Ask:

- These texts from the Synoptic Gospels emphasize the humanity of Jesus, and the text from John's Gospel emphasizes the divinity of Jesus. How do the two approaches work together to reveal the person and ministry of Jesus?

The Trial of Jesus

Read, or invite someone to read, John 18:19-24, 28-38, 19:1-16.

Call attention to the list created during the Opening Activities of the session of the events related to the trial. Circle the events that are recorded in John's Gospel. Note any events in John's Gospel that were not mentioned by the group. Discuss:

- Why did Pilate change the charge from blasphemy to insurrection?
- What is the "kingdom" that Jesus speaks about in John 18:33-37?
- What did Jesus mean when he said, "My kingdom doesn't originate from this world" and "My kingdom isn't from here" (John 18:36)?
- What does it mean for us to accept Jesus as our King?
- How do we live in the kingdom Jesus spoke about during our life on earth?

Divide once again into the three small groups. Instruct the groups to read the account of the trial in their assigned Synoptic Gospel and again note any similarities and differences with the account in John's Gospel. Scripture texts are Matthew 26:57-68 and 27:1-14; Mark 14:53-65 and 15:1-15; Luke 22:54, 63-71, and 23:1-12. (In the interest of time, suggest that individuals skim the Scriptures silently instead of one person reading the text aloud.)

Ask each group to note similarities and differences between their Gospel account and John's account. Allow time for each small group to share its findings with the whole group. Ask once again:

- These texts from the Synoptic Gospels emphasize the humanity of Jesus, and the text from John's Gospel emphasizes the divinity of Jesus. How do the two approaches work together to reveal the person and ministry of Jesus?

Invite conversation around Hamilton's observation that in this trial, Jesus was not really the one being tried, but instead it was the trial of Pontius Pilate and of the Jewish religious leaders. Discuss:

- Have you ever had to make tough decisions between your faith and the world's values? If yes, what happened?

Note that living faithfully is a process. God sends the Holy Spirit to help us discern right from wrong. The Holy Spirit is with us to grant us strength and courage to make decisions that reflect our faith. Yet, there will be times when we falter and, like Peter, deny that we even know Jesus. Remember that Jesus died for our sins. Through Christ we have forgiveness of sins and the opportunity for new life.

Passover

Read Exodus 12:21-28, which describes the first Passover meal. Share your report or a participant's report about the history and meaning of the Jewish Passover.

In the accounts of Jesus' final days, note the timing of the Passover Festival in the Synoptic Gospels in contrast to John's Gospel.

- In the Synoptic Gospels, the Passover meal was the setting for the Last Supper.
- In Matthew's Gospel, Jesus says, "I'm going to celebrate the Passover with my disciples" (Matthew 26:18).
- John sets the Last Supper and foot-washing ritual with the disciples "before the Festival of Passover" (John 13:1).
- With John's timeline, the Crucifixion occurred on the day of preparation for Passover.

Ask:

- Why was it significant for John to place the Crucifixion on the day of preparation for Passover? (sacrificial lamb)
- Why is it significant in the Synoptic Gospels that the Last Supper took place while Jesus celebrated Passover with his disciples?

Note: We do not know, historically, what the actual timeline was. We do know that Jesus chose to go to Jerusalem at the time of the Passover Festival. We can conclude that Jesus wanted his followers to understand the events of what we now call Holy Week in light of the meaning and symbolism of Passover. Passover is a celebration of God's gift of deliverance and salvation from slavery in Egypt. Jesus came for the salvation of all people.

The Crucifixion of Jesus

Read, or invite someone to read, John 19:16-30. Call attention to the list of the events related to the Crucifixion created during this session's earlier Opening Activities. Circle the events that are recorded in John's Gospel. Note any events in John's Gospel that were not mentioned by the group. Ask:

- What claim did the "public notice written and posted on the cross" make about Jesus (John 19:19)? Why was it written in three languages?
- How did the Jewish chief priests react to the claim that Jesus was "the king of the Jews" (John 19:21)?
- Why do you think Pilate identified Jesus as "the king of the Jews"? What do you imagine Pilate was thinking when he made the remark in John 19:22?
- What would you have written and posted on the cross about Jesus?

Read these words of Jesus recorded in the Farewell Discourse in John 17:1-5. Discuss:

- How was Jesus' glory revealed on the cross?
- How did Jesus glorify God through his crucifixion?

Read Exodus 12:22 and John 19:29. Ask:

- How does the mention of "a hyssop branch" add meaning to John's account of the Crucifixion? (Call attention to Hamilton's comments about this in the study book.)

Read John 19:30. Discuss:

- What did Adam Hamilton think Jesus meant by these final words? What do you think?

Divide once again into the three small groups. Instruct the groups to read the account of the Crucifixion in their assigned Synoptic Gospel and again note any similarities and differences with the account in John's Gospel.

Scripture texts are Matthew 27:32-56; Mark 15:16-41; Luke 23:26-49. (In the interest of time, suggest that individuals skim the Scriptures silently instead of one person reading the text aloud.)

Allow time for each small group to discuss its findings, then share them with the whole group. Ask:

- These texts from the Synoptic Gospels emphasize the humanity of Jesus, and the text from John's Gospel emphasizes the divinity of Jesus. How do the two approaches work together to reveal the person and ministry of Jesus?

Invite participants to share new insights, raise questions, and share experiences related to Jesus' crucifixion and the gift of salvation. If your group is large you may want to invite participants to share in pairs or small groups.

Wrapping Up

Closing Activities

John's Gospel Speaks to Us

Recall that in his opening words for this chapter, Hamilton called the arrest, trial, and crucifixion of Jesus a "dramatic climax" to the Gospel of John. Suggest that participants skim John 18–19 and refer to the three charts you made during the session to review for themselves the many events recorded by John.

Allow time for participants to reflect and journal on the three questions Hamilton posed at the beginning of the study, in light of the events of Holy Week.

- What has been said about Jesus?
- How does Jesus bring life to me?
- What response is required of me?

Participants may want to share responses, new insights, and questions they have as a result of this session together.

Encourage participants to continue the discipline of reading the Gospel of John each week.

Invite participants to share their experience of this discipline so far.

My Responses to John's Gospel

Invite participants to complete the following three sentences. If time permits, invite them to explain why they completed the sentence this way.

- One event or statement in John's account of Jesus' arrest that speaks to me is…
- One event or statement in John's account of Jesus' trial that speaks to me is…
- One event or statement in John's account of Jesus' crucifixion that speaks to me is…

Closing Prayer

Merciful God, thank you for your Son, Jesus Christ. Thank you for the amazing gifts of salvation and forgiveness. Let us always be mindful of your great love for us. Let us walk in the light of Christ with love and faith all the days of our lives. In Jesus' name we pray. Amen.

6

ETERNAL LIFE

Planning the Session

Session Goals

Through conversation, activities, and reflection, participants will:

- Examine the events in the Easter story according to the Gospel of John.
- Explore ways in which Mary Magdalene's story is our story.
- Affirm the power of the Resurrection to turn sorrow and fear into joy, hope, peace, and courage.
- Discover connections between the garden in the creation story and the garden in the Resurrection story.
- Consider how we are called to follow Christ in the work of restoring creation.
- Discern how Jesus calls us to experience heaven on earth and new life in Christ during our earthly lives.
- Celebrate the Resurrection and our hope for eternal life.
- Consider our response to the Resurrection.

Biblical Foundation

There was a garden in the place where Jesus was crucified, and in the garden was a new tomb in which no one had ever been laid. Because it was the Jewish Preparation Day and the tomb was nearby, they laid Jesus in it.

Early in the morning of the first day of the week, while it was still dark, Mary Magdalene came to the tomb and saw that the stone had been taken away from the tomb.... Mary stood outside near the tomb, crying. As she cried, she bent down to look into the tomb. She saw two angels dressed in white, seated where the body of Jesus had been, one at the head and one at the foot. The angels asked her, "Woman, why are you crying?" She replied, "They have taken away my Lord, and I don't know where they've put him."

As soon as she had said this, she turned around and saw Jesus standing there, but she didn't know it was Jesus. Jesus said to her, "Woman, why are you crying? Who are you looking for?" Thinking he was the gardener, she replied, "Sir, if you have carried him away, tell me where you have put him and I will get him." Jesus said to her, "Mary." She turned and said to him in Aramaic, "Rabbouni" (which means Teacher).... Mary Magdalene left and announced to the disciples, "I've seen the Lord." Then she told them what he said to her. (John 19:41-42, 20:1, 11-16, 18)

Before the Session

- On the board or a large sheet of paper write the heading "Easter."
- Have another section of the board or large sheet of paper available for use during the lesson.
- Have markers or chalk available to record responses from the group.
- Practice reading John 20:1-18, or several days before the session recruit someone in the group to read this passage. If you recruit a reader, give information about the setting for the reading, as described below under Bible and Book Study and Discussion.
- Collect hymnals and songbooks as needed for the closing activity, or you may choose to play recordings instead.
- Consider planning some special way to bring this study and the group's time together to a close.
- **Remember that there are more activities than most groups will have time to complete. As leader, you'll want to go over the session in advance and select or adapt the activities you think will work best for your group in the time allotted.**

Getting Started

Opening Activities

Greet participants as they arrive. Since this is the last session, make any necessary announcements related to the completion of the study. Remind participants of the importance of confidentiality.

Invite participants to reflect quietly on their past experiences of Easter, including observances and celebrations during childhood, teen years, and as adults. Some of the memories may be happy, some painful, some humorous.

Invite participants to share some of these experiences. If your group is large you may want to do this in pairs or small groups. Ask the group:

- What words and short phrases reflect or describe your experiences, understandings, impressions, and feelings related to Easter?

Instruct participants to call these out while you write them on the board or page under the heading "Easter." Invite participants to reflect on the responses you've written. What do you notice about these varied responses? For example:

- How many are joyful?
- How many reflect questions or doubts?
- How many have a secular basis (Easter baskets, candy, bunnies)?
- Among the responses, are there signs of growth or maturity in faith?

Opening Prayer

Holy God of light and life, thank you for the gift of Jesus Christ. Thank you for the Resurrection, for new life, and new possibilities. Thank you for your amazing and steadfast love. Open our hearts and minds as we study John's Gospel and explore the wonderful reality of the Resurrection. Grant us courage and direction as we share the good news of the Resurrection with others. In Jesus' name we pray. Amen.

Learning Together

Video Study and Discussion

We review John's version of the events that took place after the crucifixion and resurrection of Jesus, exploring the experience of Mary Magdalene and noting the significance of the garden in John's Gospel and in the biblical story as a whole.

After viewing the video, invite the group to discuss these questions:

- How does Jesus' empty tomb as described in John relate to Old Testament traditions about God?
- How does the fact of Christ's resurrection affect your view of death?
- How do you live differently in light of the fact that we are offered eternal life now?
- How is the way you live your life influenced by the fact that hate, sin, and death never have the final word?
- What are some of the meanings behind the image of God as a gardener in Genesis and John?
- What are some of the things you've taken away from this study of John's Gospel?

Bible and Book Study and Discussion

The Resurrection Story

In preparation for reading the Gospel passage about Jesus' resurrection, instruct participants to sit comfortably; to free their hands of pencils, papers, books, and phones; and to clear their minds of the day's concerns. After they have had time to do this, invite the group to close their eyes and listen to the Resurrection story as if they have never heard it before. Ask them to be aware of what they hear, see, and feel.

Read John 20:1-18. Take your time and read reverently, with feeling. If you have recruited another reader, invite them to read the passage.

Observe a few minutes of silence after the reading, then invite participants to open their eyes. Ask for their reactions as the story was read:

- What did you hear?
- What did you see?
- What feelings did you experience?
- What surprised you?
- What other insights or reactions would you like to share about this passage?

Mary Magdalene

Read, or ask others to read, the opening verses in the four Gospel accounts (below) that describe the women finding the empty tomb. Invite participants to note any similarities and differences.

- After the Sabbath, at dawn on the first day of the week, Mary Magdalene and the other Mary came to look at the tomb. (Matthew 28:1)
- When the Sabbath was over, Mary Magdalene, Mary the mother of James, and Salome bought spices so that they could go and anoint Jesus' dead body. Very early on the first day of the week, just after sunrise, they came to the tomb. (Mark 16:1-2)
- Very early in the morning on the first day of the week, the women went to the tomb, bringing the fragrant spices they had prepared.... It was Mary Magdalene, Joanna, Mary the mother of James, and the other women with them who told these things to the apostles. (Luke 24:1, 10)
- Early in the morning of the first day of the week, while it was still dark, Mary Magdalene came to the tomb and saw that the stone had been taken away from the tomb. (John 20:1)

Note that Mary Magdalene is the only woman mentioned by all four Gospel writers in these stories. Remind the group what we know about Mary Magdalene:

- Her name indicates that she may have been from Magdala, a town located on the coast of the Sea of Galilee.
- Luke 8:1-3 tells us that she was healed of seven demons, was one of the women who traveled with Jesus and his disciples, and helped provide for the needs of Jesus and his disciples out of her resources.
- John 19:25 tells us she was at the Crucifixion and "stood near the cross."

Discuss:

- What do you imagine Mary Magdalene's life may have been like before she met Jesus? How do you think her life was different after she met Jesus?
- How did Mary respond to Jesus' gift of healing?

- What might she have been thinking and feeling as she went to the tomb after Jesus died?

Note that Mary Magdalene's relationship with Jesus changed after the Resurrection. She recognized him not by sight, but by voice when he called her name. She responded by calling him a name she had called him during his earthly life: *Rabbouni*, which in Aramaic means "Teacher." As she fully realized the good news of the Resurrection, both her name for him and her relationship with him changed. She proclaimed to the disciples, "I've seen the Lord" (John 20:18). Ask:

- How do you respond to the story of Mary encountering the risen Christ?
- In what ways has Mary's story been your story?

The Impact of the Resurrection

Note Hamilton's point that the Resurrection has the power to transform our sorrow into joy and hope and our fear into peace and courage.

Invite participants to identify and respond to the stories of joy, hope, peace and courage that Hamilton shares in the study book.

Invite participants to identify and respond to the experiences of the afterlife that Hamilton shares in the study book.

Invite participants to share their own stories and experiences of Resurrection hope.

The Garden

Read, or invite others to read, Genesis 2:8-9; John 18:1-2; John 19:41; and John 20:15-16. Note Hamilton's observations that:

- "In the beginning" God created a garden. (Remember the opening words of John's Gospel.)
- The arrest of Jesus, one of the key events leading to the Crucifixion, took place in a garden.
- Jesus was buried in a garden.

Discuss:

- What point is the Gospel writer making by recalling creation imagery in the story of Jesus' resurrection?

- How does the resurrection of Jesus call us to the work of restoring creation to the way God intended it to be?
- What realities and forces in our world today work against the efforts of Christ's followers to restore creation?
- How have you been involved in the work of restoring creation through serving others in the name of Christ?

Heaven on Earth

Recall Hamilton's point that Jesus taught less about heaven and more about creating "heaven here on earth." Three examples of this are:

- the parable of the good Samaritan.
- the parable of the sheep and goats.
- the Sermon on the Mount.

Ask:

- How have you experienced "heaven here on earth"?
- How do you experience new life in Christ in your daily living?

Wrapping Up

Closing Activities

John's Gospel Speaks to Us

Remind participants that John's Gospel invites us into a personal relationship with Jesus Christ.

Note that one of the themes of this study has been trust. We are called to trust God.

Invite participants to reflect and journal on what they have studied in John's Gospel and how it applies in their lives.

- How have you grown in your relationship with Jesus Christ through this study?
- How have you grown to trust God more?
- What do you plan to do now in response to John's call to follow the resurrected Christ and share the good news of the Resurrection with others?

Remind participants of the goal that each person would read the entire Gospel of John during this six-week study. Since this is the last session, find out who has read the entire Gospel. Encourage those who have not completed it to do so in the coming days. Invite participants to share any insights or questions that have resulted from this experience.

Celebrate the Resurrection

If you have planned a special closing activity, do that activity with the group. If you have not, you may want to consider using songs of resurrection and new life:

- Distribute songbooks or hymnals that contain music about Easter and resurrection.
- Invite participants to select hymns and songs from the index. You might consider choosing "When We All Get Together," mentioned in the study book. Sing or read the words together.
- Alternatively, play recordings of Easter songs and hymns that you selected before the session.
- Invite participants to share phrases and ideas expressed in the hymns that have special meaning to them.

Closing Prayer

Loving God of light and life, thank you for the Resurrection. Thank you for the sure and dependable hope of salvation and eternal life. Guide and strengthen us so that we may be your faithful witnesses wherever we go. In Jesus' name we pray. Amen.

CPSIA information can be obtained
at www.ICGtesting.com
Printed in the USA
LVHW01s0024270118
564197LV00004B/4/P